A God Who Speaks

A workbook on conversational prayer

Jonathan Dillon

ISBN-13: 978-1461134015

ISBN-10: 1461134013

Contents

Foreword

W hat if your life could be different?

What if God really was like a loving Father, there in a real and present way? What if He was a God who spoke to average people? What if He spoke to *you*?

What if the holes and hurt left by your natural father could actually be filled by a new Father? What if He told you what He really thought of you? What if what He thought changed your identity so much that issues like weight, looks, relationships, and self-worth melted away? What if you actually felt a real and lasting Peace? What if you could live a life without regret?

I am consumed with the idea that this is what the Kingdom of God looks like (it's interesting that Jesus mentions the Kingdom over 50 times in Matthew). In the Kingdom of God, you have a *New Name*. You are truly and authentically free to be yourself. You are a part of something bigger—something grand—and God uses your life to further that Kingdom as it crashes into this fallen world in ways you never could have imagined. In the Kingdom of God, you are part of a great adventure. In the Kingdom of God, death is not an end.

When you hear from God, suddenly the Book of Acts looks a lot like e-mails from a friend. You can *know* who you are in Christ. You can know what His plans are for you. You are delivered from the burdens of guilt and pain. Your past does not define you. You are free—finally, truly free.

—JD,

4/27/2011

Chapter 1: Myths

When I was a child, I asked someone why it was that God no longer spoke. His reply was that God only spoke in periods of great transition, which is why we see him in Genesis, the Gospels, and in the book of Revelations. Perhaps you've heard a similar story. I think this story has been repeated so often that it has just become part of our western cultural belief system.

So...what if that story is a myth?

I guess it would be fine if myths like these didn't matter—if they held no power over us. But our beliefs shape how we see the world. Our beliefs shape how we interact with God.[1] When we believe that we serve a silent and absentee God, something changes in us. Think of a child who has never heard her father's voice, received a hug, or shared a special moment. Would this little girl have the same identity, the same sense of purpose, or a grounding of who she was at her core?

What have you heard about this topic over the course of your life?

---

[1] Mark 9:22-24

Are these beliefs grounded in Scripture or our American cultural Christianity? If Scripture, which ones?

Have these beliefs encouraged or discouraged you from attempting to hear from God?

Has this affected you and your perception of God?

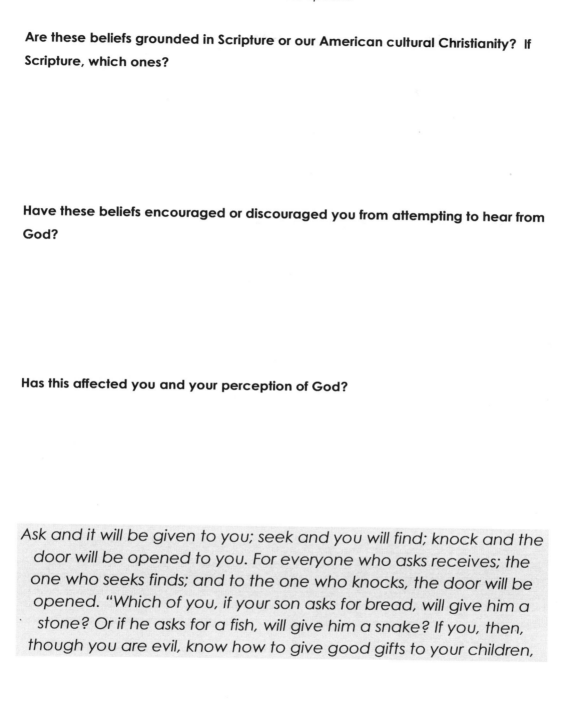

Ask and it will be given to you; seek and you will find; knock and the door will be opened to you. For everyone who asks receives; the one who seeks finds; and to the one who knocks, the door will be opened. "Which of you, if your son asks for bread, will give him a stone? Or if he asks for a fish, will give him a snake? If you, then, though you are evil, know how to give good gifts to your children,

how much more will your Father in heaven give good gifts to those who ask him!"[2]

What does this verse say about the nature of God? How does this idea reconcile with a God who doesn't speak?

God. like a good Father ~

And when Jesus had cried out again in a loud voice, he gave up his spirit. At that moment the curtain of the temple was torn in two from top to bottom. The earth shook, the rocks split and the tombs broke open. The bodies of many holy people who had died were raised to life. They came out of the tombs after Jesus' resurrection and went into the holy city and appeared to many people.[3]

When the veil ripped about the time Jesus died, what did that symbolize?

---

[2] Matthew 7:1-11
[3] Matthew 27:50-53

Chapter 2: Do all hear?

K, so we know God speaks. But...who hears, exactly? Isn't that for prophets or something?

This is a topic that I love. I love it because I know the heart of the God we serve. He loves to talk to His children. He loves when we ask for Him to show up. I firmly believe He shows up. Let me say that again: I believe in a God who always shows up. Every time.[4]

We may not be listening, we may ignore Him, we may not want to hear what He has to say...but He is always available, always willing to be there, always speaking.

> *"You have gone into the Temple...and found Him, as always, there."*
> *--CS Lewis, from a letter "To a Lady"*

It seems each person hears from God in a different way. Some have very vivid dreams, some hear a 'still, small voice,'[5] some see images, and others are given a scripture reference.

The LORD will deliver them to you, and you must do to them all that I have commanded you. Be strong and courageous. Do not be

---

[4] Hebrews 13:5; Psalm 139
[5] 1 Kings 19:12

afraid or terrified because of them, for the LORD your God goes with you; He will never leave you nor forsake you."[6]

According to Scripture, is God always with us?

If you love me, keep my commands. And I will ask the Father, and he will give you another advocate to help you and be with you forever—the Spirit of truth. The world cannot accept him, because it neither sees him nor knows him. But you know him, for he lives with you and will be in you. I will not leave you as orphans; I will come to you. Before long, the world will not see me anymore, but you will see me. Because I live, you also will live. On that day you will realize that I am in my Father, and you are in me, and I am in you. Whoever has my commands and keeps them is the one who loves me. The one who loves me will be loved by my Father, and I too will love them and show myself to them." Then Judas (not Judas Iscariot) said, "But, Lord, why do you intend to show yourself to us and not to the world?" Jesus replied, "Anyone who loves me will

[6] Deuteronomy 31:5-6

obey my teaching. My Father will love them, and we will come to them and make our home with them. Anyone who does not love me will not obey my teaching. These words you hear are not my own; they belong to the Father who sent me. "All this I have spoken while still with you. But the Advocate, the Holy Spirit, whom the Father will send in my name, will teach you all things and will remind you of everything I have said to you. Peace I leave with you; my peace I give you. I do not give to you as the world gives. Do not let your hearts be troubled and do not be afraid.[7]

Through whom will God speak according to this passage?

My sheep listen to my voice; I know them, and they follow me. I give them eternal life, and they shall never perish; no one will snatch them out of my hand.[8]

Can we know God's voice if we have never heard it before?

---

[7] John 14:15-27
[8] John 10:26-28

"Father, glorify your name!" Then a voice came from heaven, "I have glorified it, and will glorify it again." The crowd that was there and heard it said it had thundered; others said an angel had spoken to him. Jesus said, "This voice was for your benefit, not mine."[9]

Why was this for the disciples' benefit and not Jesus'?

We, in the American Church, tend to believe that the miraculous events done by Christ were done by His own power because He was God. But, Scripture might say something a little different...

But if I drive out demons by the finger of God, then the kingdom of God has come upon you[10].

So Jesus said, "When you have lifted up the Son of Man, then you will know that I am he and that I do nothing on my own but speak just what the Father has taught me."[11]

---

[9] John 12:28
[10] Luke 11:20

According to Scripture, who was the source of Christ's power?

If Jesus heard from God frequently, how did He do it?

Believe me when I say that I am in the Father and the Father is in me; or at least believe on the evidence of the works themselves. Very truly I tell you, whoever believes in me will do the works I have been doing, and they will do even greater things than these, because I am going to the Father. And I will do whatever you ask in my name, so that the Father may be glorified in the Son.[12]

So, we know that Christ performed miracles through the power of God. We also know He has passed that power on to us.

[11] John 8:28
[12] John 14:11-13

Since hearing from God is not dependent upon us, but is rather a loving gift from a gracious God, do you think it is possible for you to hear from Him?

Chapter 3: How?

I t seems that many people have unique ways to pray conversationally with God. In fact, there are many names to describe these techniques. Some terms for this type of prayer include theophostic prayer, listening prayer, and inner healing prayer. Personally, I have just started calling it 'conversational prayer' because this is one of the few terms that haven't been co-opted by a specific denomination or group.

What I love about the variations we've seen is the simple fact that God isn't predictable. If you read the Gospels, you'll find that Jesus healed people in many ways, and I suspect he did this because he knew we'd make a ritual out of it if He didn't mix it up a little.

Just now, as I was writing this section, my three-year-old little girl started crying in her bedroom after we'd tucked her into bed. I went in, and asked her what the matter was.

She replied, "I'm afraid of the dark."

In that moment, I knew the heart God has for us.

I said to her, "Baby, tonight, you'll hear from God, and you'll never have to be afraid of the dark again."

As she hugged me fiercely, I whispered to her, "God's here right now. You'll never need to be afraid again, because He'll always be there with you—even in the dark. Ask Him if this is true."

In her shaky little voice, she prayed, "God, are you here?"

I waited. It was a long minute. Suddenly, I felt the tension drain from her body. She let out a long breath.

She whispered, "He talked to me."

"What did He say?" I whispered back.

"He's here. With me."

I replied, "Is there anything else you'd like to ask Him?"

She prayed, "God...is there something scary in my closet?"

Then, faster this time, she said, "He said there is nothing scary in the closet."

Aren't those just like the questions of our secret heart? We want to know that God is real. We want to know if He'll be there for us when the chips are down. When our life is falling apart, we want to know that the God we serve will be there in a real way.

So, let's just keep it simple.

Simply ask.

Say:

"God, would you please speak to me about X?"

Expect to hear.

So, yes, go ahead. Right now. Ask Him to speak. I know you feel silly. I know you have doubts. None of that matters because we serve a God who absolutely delights in surprising His children with good things. What could be better than speaking to Him?

What did He say?

Chapter 4: Not hearing?

With believers, sometimes things seem to be a little more complicated. I am not sure why this is, but on some level I suspect our issues have a lot to do with not making Christ first in our lives. We are not passionate about seeing His kingdom realized here on Earth. With work, family, and sometimes even ministry, there is often little room for a real, vital, authentic relationship with our Savior. If we were honest with ourselves, I think we'd have to admit that we spend a lot of time building our own little kingdoms rather than His.

We worship at the twin altars of safety and comfort. We spend long hours trying to further our careers. We immerse ourselves in extra-curricular activities, or those of our families. We make business a virtue and wonder that we never hear from God (if we even have time to concern ourselves with that at all).

The steps we use to bring ourselves into alignment with God are briefly outlined below. These are the simplest, most effective steps we've found to cut through our shortcomings, weaknesses, and culture. We'll dive further into the details of each point in the following pages.

- o   Deal with spiritual realities
- o   Confess
- o   Repent
- o   Appropriate forgiveness
- o   Ask
- o   Listen

Deal with spiritual realities

When the humans disbelieve in our existence we lose all the pleasing results of direct terrorism, and we make no magicians. On the other hand, when they believe in us, we cannot make them materialists and skeptics. [13]

The greatest trick the Devil ever pulled was convincing the world he didn't exist. [14]

There are myriad books, tracts, and websites on the topic of the spiritual realm. That being said, it certainly bears review. We take a very straight-forward approach to dealing with agents of the enemy. Unlike some, we don't talk with them, ask questions, or draw out the encounter. When one finds a cockroach in the kitchen, a friendly chat seems silly when a can of pesticide or a sturdy shoe is available.

The seventy-two returned with joy and said, "Lord, even the demons submit to us in your name."
He replied, "I saw Satan fall like lightning from heaven. I have given you authority to trample on snakes and scorpions and to overcome all the power of the enemy; nothing will harm you. However, do not rejoice that the spirits submit to you, but rejoice that your names are written in heaven." [15]

---

[13] *Screwtape Letters*, LetterVII, C.S. Lewis, 1942
[14] *The Usual Suspects*, 1995
[15] *Luke 10:17-20*

Do we have authority in the spiritual realm?

> *I will give you the keys of the kingdom of heaven; whatever you bind on earth will be bound in heaven, and whatever you loose on earth will be loosed in heaven.*[16]

If we bind spiritual beings, what does Scripture say will happen?

We have had the opportunity to speak with believers all over the world. We have also had the great privilege to work with many people from different backgrounds in our ministry. Through this experience, it has become readily clear that we are right smack dab in the middle of a war. While there is much debate in Christian circles about whether believers can be possessed, oppressed or otherwise, we have found it useful to simply use the term 'demonized' to describe any condition where agents of the enemy are affecting someone's life.

---

[16] Matthew 16:19

> Then he continued, "Do not be afraid, Daniel. Since the first day that you set your mind to gain understanding and to humble yourself before your God, your words were heard, and I have come in response to them. But the prince of the Persian kingdom resisted me twenty-one days. Then Michael, one of the chief princes, came to help me, because I was detained there with the king of Persia."[17]

What does Scripture say about your prayer and the spiritual realm? Can our prayers be blocked?

The first thing we do when we begin conversational prayer is to deal with the spiritual realm in an unemotional way. We say:

> "I bind any agents of the enemy that would hinder our prayer, confuse, blind or destroy. You have no right here any longer. Leave immediately, and don't come back."

> "Does Job fear God for nothing?" Satan replied. "Have you not put a hedge around him and his household and everything he has? You have blessed the work of his hands, so that his flocks and herds are spread throughout the land."[18]

---

[17] Daniel 10:12
[18] Job 1:9-10

What does this say God has placed around Job's life?

We pray for protection for ourselves, the people we are working with, and our family. If we are in someone else's house, we ask them to pray this part. We say:

"I pray for a hedge of protection around me, my family, and my home. I pray that God would place His angels as guards at the four corners of our property."

We are especially careful to pray for health and favor in the workplace after we work with others in the area of conversational prayer. These seem to be the two places we are attacked the most.

Confess

In our culture, often confession could best be described as a litany of sins we've committed. If you are from one type of Church, you might confess these to a priest. If you're from another, you might list these to God as you pray.

Confession is always about sin. And isn't sin usually the result of lie-based thinking? I mean, really, don't we convince ourselves that what we are doing is the right thing to do at the time? Didn't we 'earn' those supplies we took from work? Didn't that person deserve to be talked about in that

Isn't confession, in its most basic form, simply stating the truth about something?

way? Or cut off while we were driving to work? Or, even flipped off? You get the point. Every time we sin—in that moment—we've justified it to ourselves with a lie. Over time, we begin to believe those lies.

In our Churches, we talk a lot about sin management. We list the things we should not do. We list the things we should do. We follow the lists. We hold each other accountable to these lists and shame each other when we fall short.

Honestly, hasn't our faith started to look a little bit like the Law? What if we didn't have to live that way? Didn't Christ come to complete and free us from the Law?

> *The heart is deceitful above all things and beyond cure. Who can understand it?*[19]

What does this say about our feelings?

If our heart is deceitful, how can we possibly know what the lie is that we believe?

> *Guide me in your truth and teach me, for you are God my Savior, and my hope is in you all day long.*[20]

From whom is the author asking guidance?

---

[19] Jeremiah 17:9
[20] Psalm 25:5

> *Let perseverance finish its work so that you may be mature and complete, not lacking anything. If any of you lacks wisdom, you should ask God, who gives generously to all without finding fault, and it will be given to you. But when you ask, you must believe and not doubt, because the one who doubts is like a wave of the sea, blown and tossed by the wind.*[21]

What does James have to say about whether God will show up? What does he caution against?

What would happen if we mistake our own feelings for God's voice? What happens if we doubt what we hear?

---

[21] James 1:4-6

Several years ago, I struggled with purity. It wasn't that I was actively sinning. It was the simple fact that I was working very hard at being pure. I was trying so hard not to look, not to see, not to think about, well...you know. I followed all of the prescriptive rules I'd been told: I had an accountability partner, the computer was in the living room, I installed accountability software on it, I etc.

It was absolutely exhausting.

One day, as I prayed, this thought crossed my mind, "Is that what freedom looks like? Shouldn't we be free in Christ?"

I asked God right then, "What is the lie I believe?"

He replied softly,

[you struggle because you believe those impure things are actually better than what your relationship with your wife could be].

Ask:

"God, will you please show me the lies I believe with regard to this area of sin in my life?"

What did He say?

At this point, we pray:

> *"God, I see now I have believed X about Y. I see that belief was a lie. Thank you for revealing this to me through your spirit."*

Pray this. How do you feel now as opposed to before?

If you still struggle with doubt, you may wish to skip ahead to the section titled "Chapter 8: Testing the Spirit".

Repent

Now that we know the lies we've believed, it's time to change our mind. That's exactly what repentance is—a changing of the direction of mind to an entirely new path. In this case, it's a change from lies to the Truth. In the New Testament, the Greek word most often used for repentance is "metanoia".

> ...metanoia *signifies a changing of the mind and heart, because it seemed to indicate not only a change of heart, but also a manner of changing it, i.e., the grace of God. For that 'passing over of the mind,' which is true repentance, is of very frequent mention in the scriptures.* [22]

> "A live body is not one that never gets hurt, but one that can to some extent repair itself. In the same way a Christian is not a man who never goes wrong, but a man who is enabled to repent and pick himself up and begin over again after each stumble—because the Christ-life is inside him, repairing him all the time." – CS Lewis, "Mere Christianity"

These words, penned nearly 500 years ago, seem almost forgotten today. Instead of trusting God to change our minds by His Spirit, we often (fruitlessly) try to change our own minds.

And, we fail.

I was shocked at God's reply, but I knew I couldn't stop there.

---

[22] "*A Disputation of Doctor Martin Luther on the Power and Efficacy of Indulgences* (The Ninety-Five Theses)," 1517

"What's the Truth? I asked. "What is the Truth I should believe?"

His answer was immediate:

[you have no idea how good your relationship with your wife can be, because you have never invited me into the bedroom]

The following verses also talk about the Truth we can have in Christ.

When the Advocate comes, whom I will send to you from the Father—the Spirit of truth who goes out from the Father—he will testify about me. And you also must testify, for you have been with me from the beginning.[23]

Who is the Advocate?

And I will ask the Father, and he will give you another advocate to help you and be with you forever—the Spirit of truth. The world cannot accept him, because it neither sees him nor knows him. But you know him, for he lives with you and will be in you. I will not leave you as orphans; I will come to you.[24]

_____

[23] John 15:26-28
[24] John 14:16-18

Who gave Him to us?

Why is He called 'the Spirit of Truth'?

So I find this law at work: Although I want to do good, evil is right there with me. For in my inner being I delight in God's law; but I see another law at work in me, waging war against the law of my mind and making me a prisoner of the law of sin at work within me. What a wretched man I am! Who will rescue me from this body that is subject to death? Thanks be to God, who delivers me through Jesus Christ our Lord! So then, I myself in my mind am a slave to God's law, but in my sinful nature a slave to the law of sin.[25]

What are our bodies' slaves to?

---

[25] Romans 7:21-24

Therefore, I urge you, brothers and sisters, in view of God's mercy, to offer your bodies as a living sacrifice, holy and pleasing to God—this is your true and proper worship. Do not conform to the pattern of this world, but be transformed by the renewing of your mind. Then you will be able to test and approve what God's will is—his good, pleasing and perfect will.[26]

What will we be able to do if our mind is renewed?

Then you will know the truth, and the truth will set you free.[27]

When we know the Truth, what does it do for us?

Would being set free change the direction of someone's life? Is this repentance?

At this stage, we pray:

_____

[26] Romans 12:1-2
[27] John 8:32

"God, I've acknowledged that I've believed X about Y. I now know that to be a lie. Would you please, in the Name of Jesus, reveal to me the Truth about the situation?"

Sincerely pray this prayer. What did God tell you?

Appropriate forgiveness

How many times have you found yourself begging for forgiveness from God? If you are anything like me, it's happened quite a bit.

I believe that this level of brokenness is good. I believe that our sin is damaging to our walk with Christ, our character, and our ministry. I believe that an important part of turning from that sin always involves a certain broken spirit.

All of that said, I wonder if our attitude toward asking God for forgiveness might be a little off.

God presented Christ as a sacrifice of atonement, through the shedding of his blood—to be received by faith. He did this to demonstrate his righteousness, because in his forbearance he had left the sins committed beforehand unpunished—he did it to demonstrate his righteousness at the present time, so as to be just and the one who justifies those who have faith in Jesus. Where, then, is boasting? It is excluded. Because of what law? The law that requires works? No, because of the law that requires faith[28].

> "We learn...that we cannot trust ourselves even in our best moments and on the other that we need not despair even in our worst, for our failures are forgiven. The only fatal thing is to sit down content with anything less than perfection." —CS Lewis, "Mere Christianity"

[28] Romans 3:25-27

When did God present Christ as a 'sacrifice of atonement?'

What did He do to those who sinned prior to this act?

Could we say then that forgiveness is not time dependent? Instead, it is dependent on…?

> *Therefore, since we have been justified through faith, we have peace with God through our Lord Jesus Christ, through whom we have gained access by faith into this grace in which we now stand. And we boast in the hope of the glory of God.*[29]

How do we gain access to this forgiveness?

_____

[29] Romans 5:1-2

> *If we confess our sins, he is faithful and just and will forgive us our sins and purify us from all unrighteousness.*[30]

From these passages we see that atonement for our sins has already been achieved. We also see that our confession of those sins frees the way for a cleansing from the Father. If you have already done the steps of Confession and Repentance, forgiveness is already yours.

At this point, we pray:

> *"Thank you God, for the work you did with Christ on the cross for our sin. I thank you for the forgiveness I already have."*

We also know that sin opens a toehold in our lives for the Evil One. These things can give him a "right of way" or the spiritual "right" to affect our lives in this area. As we've discussed before in the section titled "Deal with spiritual realities", we just need to deal with these issues matter-of-factly.

We pray:

> *"God, I know that my sin has opened opportunity in my life for the Evil One. I ask in Jesus' name that you'd remove the toehold I've given in this area. I ask you to cover me with the blood of Christ. In Jesus' name, Amen".*

There are many books available on this very subject. I'd suggest you read more on this topic if you are experiencing challenges in this area.

---

[30] 1 John 1:9

Ask

We've had a lot of build up to this point, and while I really don't want to disappoint, it's actually very simple.

We just ask:

"God, the subject of X is really bothering me right now. What would you like to say to me about this?"

Listen

We don't listen very well in our culture. Even in a conversation with a loved one, we spend more energy preparing our rebuttal than we do really focusing on what it is the other person is saying. I'm guilty of this myself.

We do the same thing in prayer, don't we? We're a bit formulaic, too. It hurts to admit it, but I'm sure that God's idea of a great conversation with His kids doesn't include the same breathy (for spiritual reasons of course) openings and endings in every conversation.

I mean, what if you talked to your husband like this?

> {breathy voice}"Dear husband, I thank you so much for what a great husband you are, and all the things you've done for our family. I'd like to ask right now, that you'd pick up some milk from the store on your way home. I know this may not be what you want right now. But, if it's your will, I'd appreciate it. I ask all these things in the name of the man who married us, Tom. I agree with myself.

Kind-of ridiculous, right? God is real. Why would we think He would enjoy a one-sided conversation like this?

I'm not saying we should be casual with God, but I am saying we should be real. And present.

I think we should invest in those conversations, and I think maybe we should invite Him to be a part of them. What if we actually spoke WITH God instead of AT Him?

So, go ahead. Ask your question.

Once you do, be still. Quiet your mind. Be quiet and really listen.

What did God say?

If you are having trouble focusing during this time, flip back to the section called "Bind your carnal mind" toward the end of this workbook.

Chapter 5: What's it like?

A couple of years ago, I was in a car accident. Even though there was no natural (or purely physical) way I could have known what would happen, I see now that I could have avoided it. I was at a stop sign and sitting there listening to my radio; my thoughts were going a million miles a minute. I was frustrated by all of the things that were pulling me in a lot of different directions.

As I waited, I felt a very specific but subtle impression: [wait]. It was very faint and I chose to ignore it. As I pulled out from the stop sign, I was struck by another car.

Now, I had the right-of-way, and I wasn't speeding...but before God, I was just as wrong as if it had been legally my fault. After all, hadn't I been told to wait?

Read the following passages:

"Father, glorify your name!" Then a voice came from heaven, "I have glorified it, and will glorify it again." The crowd that was there and heard it said it had thundered; others said an angel had spoken to him. Jesus said, "This voice was for your benefit, not mine."[31]

While he was still speaking, a bright cloud enveloped them, and a voice from the cloud said, "This is my Son, whom I love; with him I am well pleased. Listen to him!"[32]

The lamp of God had not yet gone out, and Samuel was lying down in the house of the LORD, where the ark of God was. Then the LORD called Samuel. Samuel answered, "Here I am." And he ran to Eli and said, "Here I am; you called me." But Eli said, "I did not call; go back and lie down." So he went and lay down.   Again the LORD called, "Samuel!" And Samuel got up and went to Eli and said, "Here I am; you called me."

"My son," Eli said, "I did not call; go back and lie down."

---

[31] John 12:28
[32] Mat 17:5

Now Samuel did not yet know the LORD: The word of the LORD had not yet been revealed to him. A third time the LORD called, "Samuel!" And Samuel got up and went to Eli and said, "Here I am; you called me."

Then Eli realized that the LORD was calling the boy. So Eli told Samuel, "Go and lie down, and if he calls you, say, 'Speak, LORD, for your servant is listening.'" So Samuel went and lay down in his place.

The LORD came and stood there, calling as at the other times, "Samuel! Samuel!" Then Samuel said, "Speak, for your servant is listening."[33]

After the earthquake came a fire, but the LORD was not in the fire. And after the fire came a gentle whisper.[34]

Does God speak the same way each time?

_____

[33] 1 Samuel 3:3-10
[34] 1 Kings 19:12

Is there any reason we should expect God to speak the same way each time? To each person?

Truthfully, I now have these impressions often, but it has taken me years to even hear them, let alone filter the Holy Spirit from my own internal dialogue. It has taken me so long to learn to do this because I never had anyone teach me the principles outlined below (like looking back at an event and realizing I could have listened to the Holy Spirit and avoided a lot of pain or been more effective for Christ). Hopefully, my mistakes can be a lesson for you.

Here are some high-level points that I use to help me filter.

- o it's often very faint.
- o it often *cuts across* other lines of thought
- o it tells me to do something opposite of what I want to do
- o it's never, ever wrong
- o it never goes against scripture

Now, let's look at each of these items in detail.

It's often very faint

Imagine for a moment that you are having a picnic at your house and you get stuck babysitting four active children. One is crying, another is running in circles, and a third is trying to put frosting on the cat. You don't even know where the fourth one is. Right then, if someone were to lean over and whisper 'go outside', you would probably not even hear them. If you did happen to hear them, you would probably dismiss what the individual said. You have important things to take care of, right?

This is what our thoughts are like. They run around constantly in our heads, and are usually focused on selfish pursuits.

Now...what if you looked back on that event and realized that someone had whispered 'go outside' just before your house caught fire? What if, upon further examination, you realized that there was a little whisper like that every time something happened that ended badly? Wouldn't we be more inclined to listen for that voice?

As we just read, God's voice is described in just this way:

> *And after the earthquake a fire; but the LORD was not in the fire: and after the fire a still small voice.*[35]

Often, these faint promptings are just an impression, rarely are they a full sentence or phrase.

_____

[35] 1 Kings 19:12

Look back on an event that was not beneficial, and see if there wasn't a small hint of a voice telling you to do something different. In the future, look for this just prior to making a decision. Make an effort not to override it because it is so faint. Notice those times that you ignore it. What would have happened if you hadn't?

Notice those times you listened to it—were there benefits that you could not have possibly foreseen?

As you begin the process of listening prayer, try praying with another person you trust (a spouse is often a great option). As you progress, consider asking a third person to assist you in this activity.

Pray ahead of time for God's leading. Agree together in prayer. Choose to be silent before God and individually write down what He tells you. Have the third person look at both notes (but don't let him/her share the specific results with either of you). If they match, great.

If they don't, continue until they do. This could take an hour or more. Spend the time necessary for success.

Was your prayer time more fruitful than before?

It often cuts across other lines of thought

In a past job, there was a time when I was extremely distressed. My boss told the 'top brass' that a project he neglected was mine. He then proceeded to write me up for it, even though I was innocent. That night I could not sleep. In my desperation, I tried to pray, but it was nearly impossible. I was worried about an upcoming meeting over the issue, the politics of the situation, and ultimately my job. I kept trying to pray, but I couldn't stop the whirlwind that was my thoughts. Finally, I cried out to God, "God, I can't even pray!"

Suddenly, cutting across all of my thoughts was the single message:

[TRUST ME]

A wonderful peace ensued. I was able to rest, and the meeting went so smoothly the next day that my boss was shocked. He literally sat there with his mouth open. A few weeks later, I was laid off (unrelated to the write-up) and given a severance that covered our needs perfectly until I could get my own business up and running.

If you are thinking along a particular line of thought, and an unrelated idea pops into your head, take a moment to examine it.

It may be that the Holy Spirit is trying to lead you in a direction you wouldn't naturally go on your own.

A while ago, I had one of the most rewarding conversations to date with an unbeliever about Christ. The thoughts immediately prior to this conversation went something like this: "Hmmmm. The restaurant is closed today. I am hungry. How about the Subway there. Subway is good, and kinda... [what about the bookstore]...on the lighter side...

Whoa. What just happened there? What about the bookstore? I dunno. What about it? What about Subway? Dang, I am hungry.

Bookstore you say? God, do you want me to go to the bookstore?" I focused on the bookstore and asked God if that was where He wanted me to go. I got a definite confirmation, and went in.

When I got inside, the conversation immediately turned to God, and the leading was confirmed.

Look for those times where a still, small 'voice' or impression cuts across your natural train of thought. Often these are not complete sentences. Sometimes they are just single words.

Note the impressions here:

Ask God to interrupt your prayer or thoughts with His promptings. Next time you are engaged in personal or corporate prayer, take a moment to ask God to do this. Notice when He does. Use this to 'steer' your prayer, confess a sin, or encourage another.

Note occurrences of this here:

It tells me to do the opposite of what I want

In my example above (where I outlined the less-than-flattering internal dialogue featuring the debate surrounding a sub sandwich), I illustrated the concept of God's voice telling me to do something other than what I wanted. But from a higher perspective, I think this effect should become less and less pronounced as we progress in our spiritual walk. As I grow closer to Christ, my desires will naturally start to synch with His.

If I am living for myself and I haven't had devotions in a month, I may not hear the voice of the Holy Spirit at all. On the other end of the spectrum, if I have totally surrendered myself to God, then my 'wants' will naturally parallel His, and my internal dialogue will look very different. I will become so 'distracted' by the things of God, that I may (for example) miss several meals and not even realize it.

Set up an intentional conflict in your life. For example, you could schedule ministry during your lunch break. Notice the 'impressions' you get that go opposite of what you would like to do (eat), and follow them.

Note the result.

Wait until there is something that you really want to do. It could be going to a movie, buying something, etc. Make it a point to intentionally deny yourself this thing. Pray that God will show you something else to do instead. For example, let's say I have made plans to meet a friend from church for lunch. Once you meet him/her, intentionally decide to skip this meal and do some prayer (for example) instead. Pray until you receive direction from God.

Note the result.

It's never, ever wrong

I f you ever (and, I mean ever), have one of these 'promptings' and it is wrong, there are only two possibilities: 1) it wasn't from God, or 2) it was from God but you don't have the perspective to see the benefit right now (not really wrong).

Some time ago, I was driving on a busy street. Walking along the edge of the road was a man who was clearly a Muslim. He was dressed in traditional North African clothing, complete with a turban.

I heard, "pick him up" cross my thoughts and groaned.

"God, I'm a Republican, we don't pick up hitchhikers", I prayed with a laugh.

"PICK HIM UP."

I careened into the nearest gas station, and waved him over when he walked by.

"Do you need a ride?" I asked.

"Yes," he replied, a mystified look on his face. "Why did you just pick me up? I mean, why right now?"

I stammered, and heard, "tell him". So I did.

He immediately laughed out loud. "That's great!" he said. "I was just praying to God that He'd send me a Christian to talk to. You know, Christians and Muslims have more in common than most people think. I think we need reconciliation."

From that single conversation on that blistering summer day, a ministry involving about 30 Muslims was born. The man who was walking on the road now calls himself a follower of The Way, and reads his Bible daily. I believe he is counted among those in the Kingdom of God.

Look back at promptings that you have followed and which would have seemed to be a mistake to an unbeliever.

Are there any possible outcomes from this event that God has used to draw yourself and/or others to Him? (Focus on the outcomes, not the difficulty of the circumstances.)

Think back about a decision you made that was clearly a mistake.

Was there a small voice telling you not to do it? If so, why didn't you follow it?

It never, ever goes against Scripture

As Jesus said, "a house divided cannot stand."[36] You will never be prompted to do something that is contrary to God's word. If you are, notice what that 'voice' sounds like, because it is either from yourself or from the enemy. Ignore that voice in the future. Satan 'comes as an angel of light'[37]; when tempting Jesus in the wilderness, he even quoted scripture. Don't be fooled.

One of our greatest defenses against deceptions from agents of the enemy is Scripture. We should study, know, memorize and crave it. When you receive a prompting from the Holy Spirit, search through scripture to make sure it is in line with what we as believers are called to do. You may be surprised. Many things we take for granted in our Western Christian Culture are not expressly Biblical.

As soon as it was night, the believers sent Paul and Silas away to Berea. On arriving there, they went to the Jewish synagogue. Now the Berean Jews were of more noble character than those in Thessalonica, for they received the message with great eagerness and examined the Scriptures every day to see if what Paul said was

[36] Luke 11:17
[37] 2 Corinthians 11:14

true. As a result, many of them believed, as did also a number of prominent Greek women and many Greek men.[38]

What did members of the first Century Church do when they received "new" doctrine from the Apostles?

How should we behave when we believe we have heard from God?

But a prophet who presumes to speak in my name anything I have not commanded, or a prophet who speaks in the name of other gods, is to be put to death.[39]

How serious is God about this topic?

---

[38] Acts 17:10-12
[39] Deuteronomy 18:20

Chapter 6: Other ways of hearing

We've found that God will use whatever means necessary to communicate with us. Some of the ways we've seen seem strange to our Western minds, but all are found in Scripture.

Some of the ways we've seen include:

o   Irregular Channels
o   Dreams and Visions

Let's take a look at these in depth.

Irregular Channels

One unusual way we've had God speak to us is what we call 'irregular channels'. We've borrowed this term from E. Stanley Jones. I have to admit, it's a little odd when it happens to you. By 'irregular channels' I mean any mechanism by which God chooses to speak to you that seems to fall outside of the 'normal' way to which we are accustomed (namely Scripture, other believers, etc.)

Gandhi's movement in its failure left a new spiritual deposit in the mind of India. The cross has become intelligible and vital.... "What the missionaries have not been able to do in fifty years Gandhi by his life and trial and incarceration has done, namely, he has turned the eyes of India toward the cross."[40]

Would you ever have expected to hear that Gandhi opened up parts of India for Christ?

[40] E. Stanley Jones, *The Christ of the Indian Road*, pp.77-78, 1925

The other day I was really wrestling with the fact that neither our prayer nor financial support for moving overseas was coming in. Our departure date was looming, and we were running out of time. It felt like the Church body we are a part of simply didn't care. I hate to admit it, but I was feeling sorry for myself.

Because we were so stressed, we finally decided to ask God about this. Three times, we did listening prayer on the subject.

All three times we heard:

[my timing, not your timing].

This is not the answer we wanted to hear. We wanted a miracle. We wanted it to be easy. The night after I heard it for the third time, I couldn't sleep. I had insomnia. I was upset and barely caught a couple hours of sleep.

The next day, I had a meeting with a VP at my work. She doesn't go to Church. She isn't a Christian.

As we spoke, she seemed to get agitated. Her face turned red. She fidgeted.

Finally, she said, "I need to say something to you. There is something that keeps going through my head, and I just need to say it."

I feared the worst. The way things were going lately, I was probably going to be fired. I quickly surrendered this anxiety to God and said, "Go ahead."

> She said, "I don't know how to say this."
>
> Resigned, I said, "Just say it."
>
> She blurted out, "God, or the Universe, or whatever (I don't know); says to say to you: 'IT'S MY TIMING, NOT YOUR TIMING.' Someday, you are going to have to tell me what that means."

You have to admit the God we serve certainly has a sense of humor.

> So Saul disguised himself, putting on other clothes and at night he and two men went to the woman. "Consult a spirit for me," he said, "and bring up for me the one I name." But the woman said to him, "Surely you know what Saul has done. He has cut off the mediums and spiritists from the land. Why have you set a trap for my life to bring about my death?" Saul swore to her by the LORD, "As surely as the LORD lives, you will not be punished for this." Then the woman asked, "Whom shall I bring up for you?"
>
> "Bring up Samuel," he said.
>
> When the woman saw Samuel, she cried out at the top of her voice and said to Saul, "Why have you deceived me? You are Saul!"
>
> The king said to her, "Don't be afraid. What do you see?"
>
> The woman said, "I see a ghostly figure coming up out of the earth."
>
> "What does he look like?" he asked.

"An old man wearing a robe is coming up," she said.

Then Saul knew it was Samuel, and he bowed down and prostrated himself with his face to the ground. Samuel said to Saul, "Why have you disturbed me by bringing me up?"

"I am in great distress," Saul said. "The Philistines are fighting against me, and God has departed from me. He no longer answers me, either by prophets or by dreams. So I have called on you to tell me what to do." Samuel said, "Why do you consult me, now that the LORD has departed from you and become your enemy? The LORD has done what he predicted through me. The LORD has torn the kingdom out of your hands and given it to one of your neighbors— to David. Because you did not obey the LORD or carry out his fierce wrath against the Amalekites, the LORD has done this to you today. The LORD will deliver both Israel and you into the hands of the Philistines, and tomorrow you and your sons will be with me. The LORD will also give the army of Israel into the hands of the Philistines."[41]

I am certainly not saying that consulting mediums is OK. I am, however, saying that we serve a Sovereign Lord who will use whomever He pleases to accomplish His will.

---

[41] 1 Samuel 28:8-19

I'd also like to point out that it is incredibly important to 'test the Spirit' on anything you hear through 'irregular channels'. I don't include them in this text in an effort to convince you to look for opportunities like this, but I do want you to be aware that they exist.

And we know that in all things God works for the good of those who love him, who have been called according to his purpose.[42]

Can God use 'irregular channels' according to Scripture?

Have you ever had a situation where God used "irregular channels" to speak to you?

_____

[42] Romans 8:28

Dreams and visions

H ere is an entry from my journal from a couple years ago. I hope it moves you as the experience did me.

The other night I could not sleep, so I decided to avail myself of the quiet solitude and I began to pray. I prayed for those in need, and I thanked God for all of the good things He has bestowed upon me in this life. Then, the prayer naturally progressed toward God Himself, and I thanked Him for His goodness and character. It advanced from there until I eventually meditated on Him alone.

Finally I slept, and as a matter of course, I dreamed. But then there was something different. I felt like I was taken out of that common dream to another place and time (or, conversely, it felt as though I was taken outside of all places, beyond all time). My mind was lucid—there was none of the fog or distortion common to dreams, and I experienced things as though they were happening to me (not coming from me, like a dream).

I existed. And in my existence, I was barely aware of my surroundings, for I was surrounded by a brilliant light. It was intense, and I focused inward to escape its glare. There, I saw only dim shadow compared to the life of the light. The light pulled me, and drew me with its brightness.

It was overwhelming and intense; and in its intensity, it was fierce. It was like looking at the sun—if you could look at it with your whole self, and if the light from the sun was white and pure (and if pure, purifying), and good, and complete.

The light caused a dread to fall upon me, for against it I was filthy, pitiable, and wretched. It did not condemn or measure me, but by its existence I measured and condemned myself (how could I do otherwise?). The light came from in front of me and to my left, but it had no direction (for direction implies a greater brightness in one area compared to others, and this was not the case). It surrounded me as only perfect light can, since there is no vacuum or shadow where it exists.

It was brilliant light, but it also had a physical quality to it. It touched me, and I felt its illumination. It washed over and through me, and I was overwhelmed by its purity. I

> *"I will pour out my Spirit on all people. Your sons and daughters will prophesy, your old men will dream dreams, your young men will see visions." Acts 2:17, Joel 2:28*

remember thinking, "Ah, so this is what the color white is supposed to be. What a pale, dirty thing we call our 'white'."

It was white, but it was more than white; it was the color that white imitates, like a brass trinket matched to burnished gold. It wasn't warm because it was beyond warmth. It wasn't bright because it wasn't limited by brightness. It was better, above, beyond, and behind all of these things; standing in it was like being submerged in a pool of the pure essence of love, truth, and life.

Presently, I forced my eyes up toward the light's Source. As I did, I could see the edges of something that was there—only the edges, for my eyes could not adjust to the brightness and everything looked overexposed. It was too strong (or too 'real') for me to see or process. I tried to look out of the corner of my eye, but the light was everywhere equally, and it was dazzling from all directions.

Soon, I realized that this light (the light above and behind all light I had seen or even imagined before) was not the type that could be seen with my eyes. I looked with more; I looked from within the very center of the essence of who (and what) I was.

I say 'was' because from the mere act of looking, a change began to occur. As I looked, I changed. And as I changed, I could see more. And 'the more' produced a change, and so on, until I realized that I was looking at the Source itself. As the changes happened because of the looking, I became less and less concerned with the dirtiness of myself because more and more of my mind's thoughts were consumed by Him—there was no room left for any thoughts of myself. The Light pushed every other idea out of my mind, until all that remained was the Light.

I stopped merely looking; I surrendered--and was lost in that Light.

It was then that I truly saw; and my flaws no longer mattered because all that mattered (and had ever truly mattered) was Him. I saw beyond seeing, and I was filled with pure joy at the experience. I felt fully complete for the first time in my life.

I wondered at this, and I marveled that I could be so filled with thoughts of Him. Those thoughts were so much more than my mind had ever held before; I wondered that I was not destroyed by them. I felt like a container being filled until the filling transformed it. The container became the filling, until it was lost as a container itself (for the filling cannot be contained).

I then realized that it was Him who sustained me, and allowed me to see Himself.

It wasn't me that could see, but Him in me. And, having Him in me, I was more solidly 'myself' than I ever could be without Him. I in Him, and Him in me; yet the finite 'I' was not lost even while 'in' the Infinite.

At last, when I could see clearly, I saw the figure of The Son of Man seated on a throne (and in this realization, I wondered that He had always been there, and in being there had given me the ability to see Him).

He was not just a Man, but took the form of a man. In taking that form, He drew the mass of humanity that stood before Him. A great crowd stretched out from the throne, and I could not see the end of them. There were people of all types, sizes, and colors. They were people from all places and times, and they all looked with wonder at Him—their faces awash with love, joy, and adoration. They were each clothed differently, but in spite of the revealing nature of the *light (or perhaps because of it); their robes were clean and reflected the glory of the Source.*

From Him a pure light radiated in a color that is behind the color white as a pure spring is behind (and is the Source of) a great rushing, cleansing, crystal river. It was vital, and clean, and living, and love. And, as I watched, I saw that He sat on a throne. The light was not distorted by the throne, but the illumination passed through it, and it flashed with power. This brightness shone upon the faces of those that looked toward the throne, and they reflected its light.

The figure on the throne held out His arms to the crowds before Him, and smiled at them. He was wearing a robe of the purest white.

There was something more, something written there on His thigh or on His robe (or both—I could not tell). But, just as I tried to read the words, I was taken away from that place, and the dream came to an end.

The dream felt as though it lasted moments and millennia at the same time. Even while I thought on this as I was being taken away, I understood that both were the same in that place (what is mere time to the Source, for is not time also a created thing?).

The Peace, and the Love, and the Joy, and the Hope from the dream did not end with it, but remain with me even now. And so I write this, in the hopes that it will encourage you and build your faith.

If this dream is anything like the dream of "the Man in White" that is being experienced by people around the world, I can assure you that The Way is being prepared in a powerful manner. It is so moving and so overwhelming that I am certain you will have no problems discussing Jesus Christ with any who have had this experience. For even though I know who He is, I burst with the need to share this experience. I can only imagine the distress of those who know naught of Whom they dream.

> It is best summarized: I dreamed and in dreaming, awoke. The dream was real, and exposed all the reality that had passed until the dream for a fantasy.

As I commit this dream I to paper, I agonize over every sentence, because with each statement something less is conveyed than was actually experienced. Please forgive the limits of my ability to describe this occurrence.

I've called it a dream because that is the form it took. But this experience seemed more real to me than the reality of this present 'when and where'. It made all of the reality of this life look like faint wisps of smoke in comparison with its solid realness.

It is best summarized: I dreamed; and in dreaming, awoke. The dream was real, and exposed all the reality that had passed until the dream for a fantasy.

I can tell you now that even in sitting down to record this account, I am overwhelmed at the mere memory of it. My hands shake, I've broken out in a cold sweat, and I can barely put words to paper. The recollection (as imperfect as it is) overpowers me and it moves me to the core of my being. I only hope that some small bit of the power of the experience can be transferred to you in the telling.

One other small note: this account (as feeble as it is) seems to be focused on my transformation within the dream. While that personal renovation did happen, it happened in an instant. It was nothing (in time or relevance) compared to His love, and peace, and power, and glory.

For, the real part of the dream was Him.

May all praise be to Him who WAS, and IS and IS TO COME. The AUTHOR of all. Amen.

Was this an encouragement to you? If so, in what way?

Chapter 7: Journaling

Journaling can be an especially helpful tool as you go through the process of learning to hear from God. It gives you the opportunity to record God's words to you, and it allows you to review them when a similar situation arises later. Some people are particularly suited to this, and they may have a journal or blog already in service. For me, I find journaling a chore. A nice compromise that I utilize is to simply write the date, the question, and what we heard.

We've learned some simple but important lessons on this topic over the years:

1) Only record the *exact* words you hear as the important items. The point at which we start to translate the meaning of the words is often when error creeps in. Record your feelings in a separate place. In my journal, I draw a line between the two.
2) Keep the journal with you. I keep a small Moleskine notebook in my briefcase for this purpose.
3) ALWAYS record what you hear, or you will forget.

So Joshua called together the twelve men he had appointed from the Israelites, one from each tribe, and said to them, "Go over before the ark of the LORD your God into the middle of the Jordan. Each of you is to take up a stone on his shoulder, according to the number of the tribes of the Israelites, to serve as a sign among you. In the future, when your children ask you, 'What do these stones mean?' tell them that the flow of the Jordan was cut off before the ark of the covenant of the LORD. When it crossed the Jordan, the waters of the Jordan were cut off. These stones are to be a memorial to the people of Israel forever."[43]

Do you believe that God thinks reminders of what He has done for us are important?

---

[43] Joshua 4:4-7

Chapter 8: Testing the Spirit

> *The most dangerous thing you can do is to take any one impulse of your own nature and set it up as the thing you ought to follow at all costs. There's not one of them which won't make us into devils if we set it up as an absolute guide.*[44]

s we begin to hear from God, having a way to discern whether what we hear is from Him becomes incredibly important.

Fortunately, Scripture deals extensively with this topic:

> *Dear friends, do not believe every spirit, but test the spirits to see whether they are from God, because many false prophets have gone out into the world.*[45]

What are we commanded to do in this passage?

[44] *Mere Christianity*, CS Lewis, 1952

[45] I John 4:1

Who are the false prophets warned about in this passage?

Could it be us? Are we in danger of becoming false prophets if we don't make sure we are actually hearing from God?

Do not quench the Spirit. Do not treat prophecies with contempt but test them all; hold on to what is good, reject every kind of evil[46].

What does this passage tell us to do with prophesy?

_____

[46] 1 Thessalonians 5:19-22

At this point, we pray:

"God, I believe I just heard X about Y. I need to know it is from you. I'd like to test the spirit of this word, in Jesus' name. Will you speak to me on that?"

When you receive your next prompting from the Holy Spirit, share it with a friend and have him or her check it with scripture and pray about it. Once this double check has happened, move forward.

Chapter 9: Failure

F ailure.

I really hate that word. I want to tell you that everything's easy when you hear from God. I want to tell you that you'll always hear, and what you hear will be nice.

But that wouldn't be the truth.

I have been to quite a few talks about Listening Prayer. They are frequently filled with true, inspiring stories about how God has spoken to other believers in miraculous ways.

Those meetings moved me. They motivated and inspired me.

What they didn't do was prepare me for failure. And, to be transparent, my wife and I have faced our fair share of failure. We've made mistakes. We've been disobedient. We've stopped hearing for months at a time. We've quit listening.

Sometimes it has been very, very complicated and messy.

In 1987, when I was thirteen, I spent about 3 months in Papua New Guinea with an NGO (relief agency). We were to build a hospital for those in need in the Sepik River Valley in the North lowlands. Over the course of some weeks, we ran out of food. It was then rationed.

A typical meal would consist of a thin peanut butter and jelly sandwich on stale bread accompanied by a very small scoop of canned fruit salad (perhaps a tablespoon). For a teenager working construction, this was not nearly enough calories.

Soon, my weight plummeted to 132 pounds, my hair turned orange, and my energy waned. Lethargy defined my actions. I had trouble focusing. I remember at one point becoming confused as to where I was or why I was there. I believed I had always lived in a little tent in the bush, and I couldn't remember what my family looked like. I'd forgotten the faces of my parents.

Fast-forward to several years ago. In my very first experience with listening prayer, I found myself faced with four big issues in my life. One of them was my weight. I was clinically obese. During this first experience hearing from God, I laid this issue (along with the three others) on the altar in prayer.

I heard, [all of these issues are issues you have with Me].

"What?"

I asked, "What issue do I have with you?"

He replied, [you don't trust Me.]

I replied, a bit indignant, "Of course I do, you're God."

[you trust me with your head, but not in your heart. you don't know you can trust Me. what do you hear?]

I stammered in the prayer in my mind, "What?"

[what do you hear when you eat?]

I thought about it for what seemed like hours. Finally, I asked Him to reveal the Truth to me, and it dawned on me. When I ate breakfast that morning, I heard in my head, "Fill up, you don't know if you are going to get lunch." At lunch, I heard, "Fill up, you don't know if you are going to get dinner." At dinner, I heard, "Fill up, you don't know if you are going to eat tomorrow." I'd heard this for years, and ate every meal as if it was my last. I overate because I really didn't believe that God would provide the next meal for me.

As I prayed, God revealed to me a deeper issue: Hadn't I gone without? Hadn't I gone without while actively serving Him? Where was He then?

When I asked Him to reveal the lie I believed, He replied, [you believe I abandoned you when you were serving Me.]

I whispered, "What's the Truth, then?"

In my mind, it was as though I felt His arms around me. I felt Him step forward as a father would do for a hurt child. That contact transformed me.

He said, [I was there with you.]

Suddenly, for the first time in my life, I knew in my heart (not just in my head) that God was good. Actually truly and fully good. He wanted the best for me. I could trust Him.

He brought to mind that I didn't starve. Sure, I was uncomfortable. But He did provide for me. It wasn't what I wanted but it was what I actually needed.

After this revelation, I began to lose weight. I trusted God for my next meal. It changed my outlook on life. It transformed me.

But.

It's not that simple. Life's complicated, remember?

Soon, I hit a plateau. My weight loss stopped. I prayed about it, and God brought someone into my life who recommended I see a doctor about the constant nausea I was experiencing (and eating to assuage). I did, was prescribed medication, and my weight loss continued.

But.

Soon, I hit another plateau.

Being overweight is incredibly painful in our culture. If you are overweight, you know what I'm talking about. People mention it all the time. They assume you are lazy or lack self-discipline. Research shows that overweight people make less money and are passed up for promotions. The ministry agency we work with actually called out my weight during the assessment process. They told me they would conditionally accept me as an associate only if I lost weight.

The justification for these bullying behaviors is always, "…but you can help it!"

Let me be clear. I truly don't believe this is a self-control issue in my life. I've prayed on it, and my wife will confirm this.

I tried every diet I could. I'd lose a little weight but I'd never be able to keep it off. My frustration was compounded by the fact that my wife weighs 110 pounds and I have similar eating habits. Still, I struggle. I've been to doctors. I've had accountability partners. I've counted points, calories and weighed everything. I still gain weight. One doctor told me I'd need to eat less than 1500 calories a day for the rest of my life if I wanted to be thin.

> "What can you ever really know of other people's souls — of their temptations, their opportunities, their struggles? One soul in the whole of creation you do know: and it is the only one whose fate is placed in your hands."
> ---CS Lewis, *Mere Christianity*

I spoke about listening prayer to a young man I was working with at work. A co-worker who sat next to me overheard the conversation and was intrigued. I went over the basics with her, and a couple days later she came in absolutely glowing.

"I heard from God!" she gushed.

"Great," I said, "what did He talk to you about?"

"Uh, uh." She replied with a smile, shaking her head. *"You told me not to tell. Why don't you ask God what He spoke to me about?"*

And so I did a couple days later. I heard, [it was about your weight].

I went back to work and told her it was about my weight. She was shocked to say the least. She had heard that God was allowing me to go through this for this season for His own reasons.

Later, when I placed this subject before Him, I heard, [I've allowed you to be overweight because you judge others].

When I examined my heart, I found that was true. I was extremely critical of others. I judged people constantly. I was especially hard on people who...ironically...were overweight. I treated them like they were undisciplined. Like they were lazy. Like they were gluttons. In spite of all my own problems, I had set myself above them.

> *Victorious living does not mean freedom from temptation, nor does it mean freedom from mistakes.*
> *--E. Stanley Jones*

I fell to my knees and repented of my behaviors. I asked God to set a guard before my mind. I asked Him to help me see people as Christ does. This single act transformed my relationships. I was able to finally accept people for who they were. I could want the best for them, without imposing my version of 'the best'. I could let them *progress in their walk with Christ at their pace, not mine. I could see all of their strengths in spite of their shortcomings. I could finally be the Face of Christ to others in a way never possible before.*

> *You cease to move into yourself, away from others. You give up your antagonism. You begin to move toward others in love. God moved toward you in gracious, outgoing love, and you move toward others in that same outgoing love.*
> *--E. Stanley Jones*

At the time of this writing, I still struggle with my weight. People still criticize me often for it (many of them believers). But now, I am able to love them. I am able to see their strengths. I am able to sort the important things from things that don't matter. I am able to love them in spite of their faults.

None of this was neat. None of it was tidy, and none of it was easy. But, throughout this entire experience, God has used my weakness to perfect His work in me. And, in doing so, He has given me relationships with a depth and richness I would not have been able to appreciate without this issue.

God has used my imperfections for His glory.

Through all of our failures and missteps, God has been faithful. From those failures, we have learned a huge deal about the goodness of God, His character, and His faithfulness.

We've also started to figure out why we haven't heard. As you review the list below, please realize this isn't exhaustive, nor is it complete. It is simply a list of actual items we've come across in the last few years. I'm sure this list will continue to grow as we grow in Christ.

Main reasons why we "don't hear":

- o Sin
- o Disobedience
- o Hold/Wait*[47]
- o Maintain Course*
- o Wrong Question*
- o Surrender

---

[47] Items marked with an * indicate a perceived silence when none actually exists.

Sin

Sin is huge.

We fight it all the time. It's subtle. It permeates our thinking. It surrounds us in this fallen world. Sin also prevents us from hearing God.

We know that the law is spiritual; but I am unspiritual, sold as a slave to sin. I do not understand what I do. For what I want to do I do not do, but what I hate I do. And if I do what I do not want to do, I agree that the law is good. As it is, it is no longer I myself who do it, but it is sin living in me. For I know that good itself does not dwell in me, that is, in my sinful nature. For I have the desire to do what is good, but I cannot carry it out. For I do not do the good I want to do, but the evil I do not want to do—this I keep on doing. Now if I do what I do not want to do, it is no longer I who do it, but it is sin living in me that does it.[48]

What does Scripture say about Sin?

Everyone who does evil hates the light, and will not come into the light for fear that their deeds will be exposed. But whoever lives by

---

[48] Romans 7:14-20

the truth comes into the light, so that it may be seen plainly that what they have done has been done in the sight of God.[49]

What might keep us from wanting to hear from God?

One particularly subtle and destructive sin that we've found is bitterness or lack of forgiveness. You can see the problems it caused for me in my story about weight loss (I harbored resentment toward God, resulting in a skewed perception of Him).

We'll cover more on forgiveness later, but let's just look at one critical point here:

For if you forgive other people when they sin against you, your heavenly Father will also forgive you. But if you do not forgive others their sins, your Father will not forgive your sins.[50]

How serious do you think God takes this sin?

If we sense that our failure to hear is due to a sin issue, we simply ask:

_____

[49] John 3:20-21

[50] Matthew 6:14-15

> *"God, in Jesus' name we ask that you'd show us areas of sin in our lives. Please especially reveal areas that could be keeping us from hearing from you."*

This process can take hours. Once you have heard from God about the sin in your life, go back to the Confession and Repentance stages again and start over.

Disobedience

We've found that much like ongoing sin, a refusal to obey in a specific area will also result in a loss of communication with God. In short, we don't get another set of instructions until we've followed that last set of directives. Conversational prayer is not for chitchat.

Our Father is a Sovereign God. His name will be glorified. He desires for all people to be in the Kingdom of God. We hear best when we are in line with His purposes in this area.

I remember once when I was working with a friend on this, he came to me and described his experience:

He was praying with a few other believers, and he felt God was saying a couple rather random things to him. These things included the words, "green", "bird", and "library".

As he continued to pray, he felt the strong impression to leave immediately. He did, and went to the library near the college campus.

Just as he arrived, a young man walked out of the front door wearing a green T-shirt on with a bird on the front. My friend was nervous and froze, even though he knew God wanted him to share Christ with this young man.

He left with an abject feeling of failure. And, he quit hearing from God.

By the time we talked, he was distraught. His sleep was disrupted, his quiet times were meaningless, and he felt empty.

As he spoke, I felt led to say this prayer: "Lord, you know my friend. He wants to serve you. He's confessed and repented from the sin of disobedience. Would you please, in Jesus' name, redeem that opportunity?"

He left feeling better, but a bit dubious.

I didn't see him for a couple days, and when I did he was absolutely glowing. I knew something great had happened.

When I asked him, he replied, "I did listening prayer again. I heard, 'Library, NOW.' I obeyed immediately. When I got there, there was the same guy coming out of the front door. I was able to share Christ with him."

Scripture says God is separated from us when we disobey.

But your iniquities have separated you from your God; your sins have hidden his face from you, so that he will not hear.[51]

Think back to a time when you were walking in disobedience. Do you think you would have heard from God during this time?

_____

[51] Isaiah 59:2

Prayer is co-operation with God. It is the purest exercise of the faculties God has given us - an exercise that links these faculties with the Maker to work out the intentions He had in mind in their creation.[52]

Have you had a time where you felt distant from God because you did not follow something you knew He wanted you to do?

Describe the experience here:

_____

[52] E. Stanley Jones

Hold/wait

Sometimes, when we've asked to hear from God, we haven't gotten an answer. But we didn't have the feeling of separation we'd experienced in the past because of sin or disobedience.

This condition used to bother me quite a bit until I realized it wasn't that God was silent, it was just that He was telling us to [wait] for now.

The good news is that usually when this idea occurs to us, and we ask, God often answers immediately.

We ask:

> *"God, we feel like are not hearing from you right now. Is that because you are actually telling us to 'wait'?"*

Maintain course

This is very similar to the condition just outlined (hold/wait), except this situation applies to those who are currently in a pattern of active obedience or movement.

Often, when we are in the middle of a ministry venture, when God is working through us, He has provided Divine Appointments, and we are being obedient...we don't tend to receive a new set of "marching orders" until that season has passed.

If you find yourself in this situation, just continue to move forward until such time as you need a new set of directions; you'll get them then. For related information, look over the section titled "Let's talk about faith...again" at the end of this work book.

Wrong question

When I lay these questions before God I get no answer. But a rather special sort of 'No answer.' It is not the locked door. It is more like a silent, certainly not uncompassionate, gaze. As though He shook His head not in refusal but waiving the question. Like, 'Peace, child; you don't understand.'[53]

Y ou know, we are such fallible creatures. We think so highly of ourselves, and yet next to God's Holy Righteousness our best works are shabby at best. As I learn more about this process, it has been made clear to me that many of the questions I asked in the past were very self-focused and shallow.

The following passage was used by a friend to challenge me on some of my beliefs:

"Lord," Martha said to Jesus, "if you had been here, my brother would not have died. But I know that even now God will give you

Can a mortal ask questions which God finds unanswerable? Quite easily, I should think. All nonsense questions are unanswerable.
---CS Lewis, A Grief Observed

whatever you ask." Jesus said to her, "Your brother will rise again." Martha answered, "I know he will rise again in the resurrection at the last day." Jesus said to her, "I am the resurrection and the life. The one who believes in me will live, even though they die; and whoever lives by believing in me will never die. Do you believe this?" "Yes, Lord," she replied, "I believe that you are the Messiah,

---

[53] CS Lewis, A Grief Observed, 1961

the Son of God, who is to come into the world." After she had said this, she went back and called her sister Mary aside. "The Teacher is here," she said, "and is asking for you." When Mary heard this, she got up quickly and went to him. Now Jesus had not yet entered the village, but was still at the place where Martha had met him. When the Jews who had been with Mary in the house, comforting her, noticed how quickly she got up and went out, they followed her, supposing she was going to the tomb to mourn there. When Mary reached the place where Jesus was and saw him, she fell at his feet and said, "Lord, if you had been here, my brother would not have died." When Jesus saw her weeping, and the Jews who had come along with her also weeping, he was deeply moved in spirit and troubled. "Where have you laid him?" he asked. "Come and see, Lord," they replied. Jesus wept. Then the Jews said, "See how he loved him!" But some of them said, "Could not he who opened the eyes of the blind man have kept this man from dying?"[54]

In these verses, what does Martha talk about? How does Jesus answer her?

---

[54] John 11:21-37

Was her focus on this world or the next?

What was Jesus focused on?

We, like those that commented in verse 36, often think that Jesus' sorrow is due to the loss of a dear friend.

But, I wonder. I wonder if this Man who came to transform our world, to give Himself for us, to reconcile us with a Just God, was moved because we still didn't get it. After all of the preaching, the miracles, the discourse about the Kingdom of God, and all we want is for Him to raise someone from the dead.

It's like He was saying, "Guys, the Kingdom of God is available to you here and now. This Kingdom is so different than anything you've known before. It transcends death. You can have true lasting peace. It will revolutionize your life...and all you can think about is raising someone from the dead? I'm right here. Right now. In front of you."

That idea reminds me of another story. Jesus and the disciples are crossing a lake. Jesus, tired, falls asleep in the bottom of the boat. Suddenly a storm kicks up, and it's apparently pretty serious because the disciples start to freak out. This is significant because as fishermen, they'd seen storms before. In addition, they are in the boat with Jesus Himself.

The disciples went and woke him, saying, "Lord, save us! We're going to drown!" He replied, "You of little faith, why are you so afraid?" Then he got up and rebuked the winds and the waves, and it was completely calm. The men were amazed and asked,

> *"What kind of man is this? Even the winds and the waves obey him!"*[55]

Sometimes we've asked about things that were really important to us. During difficult financial times we wanted to know about losing our house. We wanted to know about having another child (after a painful miscarriage). We wanted to hear where the next rent payment was coming from.

All we heard for weeks was:

[pride]

God used (not caused) those very painful life experiences to transform my heart from one filled with pride to one defined by humility. He wasn't concerned with all of those other things because (as we found out later), He already had set events in motion to solve those issues.

He cared more about my character than my comfort.

If you find yourself in the situation where you are not hearing from God, consider that you might actually be asking the wrong question. Could it be that He is more worried about your heart than your weight? Could it be that He wants to form you into a person more like His Son more than He needs you in that ministry that consumes all of your time?

Once, the only thing God wanted to talk to my wife about was that He wanted her to stop watching a particular TV show.

Now, we pray:

> *"God, I'm not hearing from you on subject X. Is there anything, on any subject, that you'd like to talk to me about?"*

---

[55] Matthew 8:25-27

How is it that people who are quite obviously eaten up with Pride can say they believe in God and appear to themselves very religious? I am afraid it means they are worshipping an imaginary God. They theoretically admit themselves to be nothing in the presence of this phantom God, but are really all the time imagining how He approves of them and thinks them far better than ordinary people: that is, they pay a pennyworth of imaginary humility to Him and get out of it a pound's worth of Pride towards their fellow-men.[56]

56 "Mere Christianity" CS Lewis, 1943

Surrender

The final reason we've found that we do not hear is that we haven't surrendered properly to God's will. This one is extremely tough. The challenge is that we are really good at kidding ourselves that we are completely surrendered when in reality we haven't surrendered anything.

Surrender cannot be partial.

Surrender cannot hold something in reserve.

Surrender cannot hold *anything* in reserve.

This includes your family, job, future, retirement, looks, self-esteem, ministry, finances, etc.

A good barometer for surrender is your emotions. We've found that we simply cannot pretend that we've completely surrendered our will to God's when we are anything but emotionally neutral about the outcome. This became painfully obvious to us after we petitioned God for an answer on having another child after a very painful series of miscarriages.

> *If you're approaching Him not as the goal but as a road, not as the end but as a means, you're not really approaching Him at all.*
> *---CS Lewis, A Grief Observed*

We had to deal with anger, hurt, sadness and other emotions to get through this time. But in the end, after we were able to finally surrender our desires to God, a true peace ensued like we had never experienced before.

Of course there was still pain. But there also was Christ. We still preferred to have another child, but this was tempered by an even stronger desire for God and a nearly tangible need to see His will done on earth...no matter the cost.

Another important key is to check your motivation for asking a question. In our case, we found that we wanted to know answers to questions like, "where is the rent coming from?" because we really didn't want to live by faith. We didn't want to trust that God would provide for us, and we didn't want to surrender control of our finances to Him.

Once we did however, a marvelous peace ensued, and the question became unimportant.

> I appeal to you therefore, brothers, by the mercies of God, to present your bodies as a living sacrifice, holy and acceptable to God, which is your spiritual worship.[57]

Take a moment to self-reflect. Ask God to reveal to you areas you need to surrender to Him. What are they?

> You Samaritans worship what you do not know; we worship what we do know, for salvation is from the Jews. Yet a time is coming and has now come when the true worshipers will worship the Father in the Spirit and in truth, for they are the kind of worshipers the Father seeks. God is spirit, and his worshipers must worship in the Spirit and in truth.[58]

If we know that total surrender is an act of worship, how important is it that we be completely honest and through with this?

---

[57] Romans 1:1

[58] John 4:22-24

Can we "discover the Truth" on our own? If not, who can reveal this to us?

There are two kinds of people: those who say to God, "Thy will be done," and those to whom God says, "All right, then, have it your way."[59]

What type of relationship do you think the second type of person has with God?

If the Holy Spirit can take over the subconscious with our consent and cooperation, then we have almighty Power working at the basis of our lives, then we can do anything we ought to do, go anywhere we ought to go, and be anything we ought to be.[60]

How does this apply to you?

_____

[59] *The Great Divorce*, CS Lewis 1945

[60] *"The Christ of the Indian Road"* E Stanley Jones 1925

The terrible thing, the almost impossible thing, is to hand over your whole self—all your wishes and precautions—to Christ.[61]

Do you think you can do this with Christ's help?

[61] *"Mere Christianity"*, CS Lewis 1943

Chapter 10: *Still* not hearing?

I f you are still not hearing from God, I'm sure you are pretty frustrated at this point. First, I'd encourage you to go back and work through the steps specifically surrounding the concepts of confession and repentance. This usually works.

If it doesn't, keep reading.

- o bind your carnal mind
- o loosen communication
- o borrow faith
- o ask for a divine appointment

Bind your carnal mind

The adventure has been interesting. God has slowly been working on me on all of the prior topics over the last couple of years, but an interesting surprise came when I visited some friends working in the Middle East. As we began to share our experiences with each other, it became immediately apparent that God had shown us nearly the exact same steps at about the same time. We just sat there and grinned at each other as we outlined God calling us to sell everything we owned and called us to a life of surrender.

One thing that God had revealed to them that we hadn't known about was a solution to the problem of an 'over-active' mind during prayer. I guess they just couldn't still their minds when they were trying to hear from God, and their prayer life suffered as a result. After much prayer and fasting, God told them to "bind their carnal mind" in Jesus' name.

I will give you the keys of the kingdom of heaven; whatever you bind on earth will be bound in heaven, and whatever you loose on earth will be loosed in heaven. [62]

Does Scripture support this idea?

I Tested the Spirit on this particular technique, and after much prayer, we tried it for ourselves. The results were amazing. Finally, we could focus on God instead of the kids, the bills, work and other worries.

---

[62] Matthew 16:19

We say:

> *"God, I can't seem to focus. In Jesus' name I bind my carnal mind, and order it to be silent."*

Loosen communication from Heaven

In the previous section, we covered the topic of 'Binding Your Carnal Mind.' As I focused on this idea, and prayed over it...another idea kept coming to me. See, we were able to focus on God now. But, we still weren't hearing. We were going through a dry spell.

Focusing was great, but when we weren't hearing anything, it made the silence all the worse. Even a few minutes of real silence can be weird.

Anyway, as we prayed about this, the only thing I kept hearing was:

[loosen]

"What!?" I'd ask. And, I'd just hear:

[loosen]

"Huh?"

So, I prayed about this for a few days. Finally, the verse below came to me:

> *I will give you the keys of the kingdom of heaven; whatever you bind on earth will be bound in heaven, and whatever you loose on earth will be loosed in heaven.*[63]

Write your thoughts on this verse.

[63] Matthew 16:19

Do you really think this scripture is literal?

"What?", I asked God (and yes, I ask that a lot). And I heard:

[loosen it]

So, I did. Together, kneeling in front of our couch, I prayed with my wife:

"In Jesus' name, I loosen communication from Heaven. I loosen it in the name of Jesus Christ."

Suddenly, it was like we had turned on the tap. I got answer after answer. Aimee got the same answer each time. We know this because we wrote them down individually.

That night, God answered twelve different prayers for us out of His mercy. Twelve. At one time.

If you are struggling with hearing from God, I'd encourage you to loosen the communication in Jesus' name.

See what happens.

Borrow faith

T he idea of faith has always seemed to be a bit odd to me. I've always been painfully aware that I didn't have much. Of course, Scripture says we don't need much, but that always discouraged me more than anything else. After all, if I could move mountains with faith the size of a mustard seed,[64] how miniscule must mine be? Seriously. I couldn't even trust God with my hair loss issues, let alone something important.

So, if I don't have faith…and nothing ever happens (because I don't have enough faith) how am I supposed to have the faith required to trust God make big things happen? Ugh. Wasn't that a catch-22?

Then something changed in my life, and from that moment on, faith wasn't an issue.

What happened?

Well, someone shared their faith with me. I'm not talking about this term like we usually mean it (where someone goes around with a little tract and knocks on doors). I mean someone actually *shared their faith with me*.

Once, I was attending a conference and the speaker stood up and talked about listening prayer. I, being the logical guy that I am, prepared myself to zone out for the next 20 or so minutes until she finished her talk.

But, she didn't let me off the hook so easily. She asked us all to bow our heads (right then and there) and walked us literally through many of the steps outlined within these pages.

I expected an emotional plea.

But it was nothing like that. It was logical. Straight forward. Brief.

---

[64] Matthew 17:20

I was surprised that she just stood there—in front of all of us, and expected God to actually, literally speak to me. Like she'd expect to hear from a guest speaker. I laughed a little to myself. I found it a little sweet. And naïve.

I found it sweet and naïve, that is, until I actually heard God.

God.

Speaking to me.

Telling me what He thought of me. Telling me what my heart issues were. Breaking through all the defenses I had. Defenses of logic, theology and doctrine.

He spoke to me because she shared her faith. She let me use it for a few minutes. And, after that, I had some of my own to lend. Because when you hear from God, something changes inside of you. You know, that you know, that you know.

It isn't head knowledge anymore. It's heart knowledge. And, heart knowledge comes with a measure of faith built in.

Some men brought to him a paralyzed man, lying on a mat. When Jesus saw their faith, he said to the man, "Take heart, son; your sins are forgiven".[65]

Did these men share their faith with a failing friend?

_____

[65] Matthew 9:2

How?

> *"It has often thrown him into fire or water to kill him. But if you can do anything, take pity on us and help us." "'If you can'?" said Jesus. "Everything is possible for one who believes." Immediately the boy's father exclaimed, "I do believe; help me overcome my unbelief!" When Jesus saw that a crowd was running to the scene, he rebuked the impure spirit. "You deaf and mute spirit," he said, "I command you, come out of him and never enter him again."*[66]

What does Jesus say is possible with faith?

If you find yourself in a similar state to the one I was in when I started this process, I'd suggest you ask God for the faith you need. After that, find someone to share theirs with you. If that's not available, then borrow mine. Know this: every single story in this workbook is real, understated, and as accurate as I can make it.

Expect the same, and you'll have it.

---

[66] Mark 9:22-25

Ask for divine appointments

Here's the thing. We really care about this world. And, newsflash: things that are important to us may or may not be important to God.

We care about jobs, homes, and good schools for our kids.

We ask for these things. Sometimes, it's all we talk about to God.

We care about retirement, status, and income.

God is not like that. He cares about our character. He is passionate about you. He is also passionate about the lost.

Let me explain it this way:

Imagine you have two kids, and you go to the park on a sunny Saturday afternoon. It's beautiful. You love spending time with your kids. You couldn't be happier.

But while you are there, one child gets lost. Now imagine you start looking for the lost child and your first child starts asking for an ice cream cone. The child goes on and on and simply won't stop asking.

"Help me find your sister!" you plead.

> *Prayer is commission. Out of the quietness with God, power is generated that turns the spiritual machinery of the world. When you pray, you begin to feel the sense of being sent, that the divine compulsion is upon you.*
> *E Stanley Jones*

Instead your child starts to cry. She screams, "I want a strawberry ice-pop, RIGHT NOW—you promised!"

How much of a priority is the ice cream cone to you right now? I mean you love to bless your children with treats, but isn't the lost child a little more important?

Isn't this how God must feel? He cares about us, but He also cares about the billions of lost who will never be reconciled to Him. And...all we want to talk about is that receding hairline or the promotion at work?

I've found one prayer that God always answers. Right away, every time:

"God, in Jesus' name would you please give me an opportunity to share Christ with someone today? Will you please use me; even use me up, to reach someone for the Kingdom of God? Will you let me be the face of Christ to a hurting person?"

Pray it. And you'll have a little faith to share.

Pray it, and be prepared to be blessed.

Chapter 11: Parting Thoughts

On the nature of God

Much of the difficulty we face as Westerners in the area of conversational prayer seems to fall under two loose headings: a love for our cultural Christian religion (over our love for God Himself) and a gross misunderstanding of the nature of God.

After you begin to hear from God, you'll understand the first pretty well. It'll be painful to admit, but you'll get it.

But the second topic can be one that actually prevents us from hearing from Him. That's a problem. See, we either wrap God up in a tidy little fun package like Santa Claus, or we've placed on His shoulders all the faults of all the leaders we've known who failed.

> *"We're not necessarily doubting that God will do the best for us; we are wondering how painful the best will turn out to be."* -- CS Lewis

Neither view is accurate.

We create for ourselves either a pre-occupied, distant God (with whom we have no possibility therefore no responsibility for a real relationship), or a petty, vengeful God we don't respect.

In either case, we don't trust Him. And our lack of trust has planted a seed in our hearts. A seed that has blossomed into a thistle called 'Independence'. We don't need Him. We can do it.

But God isn't weak or distant. He isn't absent or silent.

God is Sovereign. And Just. He is In All Time. He Is Everywhere. He Is Perfect. And Holy. Complete. Without End. Loving, Faithful, Merciful and Great.

And...worthy of our trust.

We don't get to create the god we want. We need to correct our view of the God that is. And, if you are like me, you won't be able to do this yourself.

> *"'Safe?' said Mr. Beaver...'Who said anything about safe? 'Course he isn't safe. But he's good. He's the King, I tell you.'" ---CS Lewis, "The Lion, The Witch and The Wardrobe"*

One of my first prayers was:

"God, are you a good God? Can I trust you? Can you please show me that you are good?"

There is nothing wrong with this honest prayer. I'd suggest you pray it. I think you will be moved at what you hear.

Sharing what you hear

When we first began to hear from God, it was amazing. We saw healings. We had Divine Encounters. Our outreach excelled. People came into the Kingdom of God.

Because of this, many people asked us to pray with them. All but one or two heard from God. But then, things changed. People started to ask us to pray for them...a lot.

From the very first time, God told us not to tell them what we heard. And, we didn't understand it. After all wasn't it about them? Wasn't it important?

We didn't understand then what we know now.

First, many people will ask others to pray for them because it is simply easier than doing the work themselves. I mean, who wouldn't want custom answers hand-delivered on demand (without having to confess, repent, or any of that other tiresome work?)

Second, if you tell people the answers they seek, you become like a conduit from them to God, but worse than that. You actually get between them and God. You become their prophet or priest or whatever.

So. Even if you are well-intentioned, if you tell people what you hear from God on their behalf, you stand between them and God and you prevent them from growing or hearing themselves.

Now what we do is pray for people and offer to confirm what God said once they hear. When we hear, we simply tell them "We've heard from God about your situation. Once you hear from God, let us know and we'll let you know when it's the same thing."

If they hear something different, we don't tell them they are wrong (unless it is anti-scriptural or God tells us to); we just tell them we've heard something different. We wait to confirm what they've heard until it matches exactly...but we don't let them guess at it.

Settling your mind

There are a couple ways that help me focus when I am trying to hear from God. One thing I like to do is acknowledge the items that are pre-occupying my attention, and then visualize placing those items in a box and placing them at the foot of the cross. I say:

> *"God, I surrender these things to you. Will you please carry this load for me? I can't do it myself."*

It's amazing how well that works.

Second, with people who are new to conversational prayer, I usually just tell them to pray about those items the way they normally would. There is nothing wrong with this, and this ritual will often will help soothe their nerves. As people gain experience in this type of prayer, I'd wean them from the formulaic style when you can.

> *"Come to me, all you who are weary and burdened, and I will give you rest. Take my yoke upon you and learn from me, for I am gentle and humble in heart, and you will find rest for your souls. For my yoke is easy and my burden is light."*
> *--Jesus of Nazareth*

If these don't work, go back to "Binding Your Carnal Mind."

Pursuit of happiness

I know this is a bit of an odd topic to add to a book on prayer, but because it comes up so much in our ministry to Americans, we feel compelled to include it here.

We frequently hear, "But I just want to be happy."

The person who says this is often miserable, self-absorbed and spiritually bankrupt. Unfortunately, this idea permeates the very core of our society.

> *"All that we call human history--money, poverty, ambition, war, prostitution, classes, empires, slavery--[is] the long terrible story of man trying to find something other than God which will make him happy." --CS Lewis, "Mere Christianity"*

Unfortunately, Happiness is one of those intangible feelings that simply cannot be satiated by its pursuit. Modern science tells us that feelings are a result of behavior, and I'd opine the opposite should be true: behavior should not be dictated by feelings.

Jesus talks about this concept when He tells us to "...love your neighbor as yourself." He is not talking about making yourself feel nice about someone, He is telling you to act the way you would if you did.

[The natural life] knows that if the spiritual life gets hold of it, all its self-centeredness and self-will are going to be killed and it is ready to fight tooth and nail to avoid that.[67]

We, as Americans, call it "pursuit of happiness". God just calls it selfishness.

---

[67] "*Mere Christianity*", CS Lewis, 1943

Selfishness is sin.

So. If you want to hear from God, you'll need to surrender your "rights". You'll need to give up your pursuit of happiness. You'll need to pursue God.

God can't reveal the full plan…

For our future to us because we'd freak out. Yep, I'm sure of it. When I first heard from God, I wanted to know the Big Plan. I wanted to know what He had in store for us, maybe in a nice chart format, with milestones at the one-, five- and ten-year highlights. Microsoft Project would be nice, too, and then I could plot the Critical Path…

But, He knew me better than that.

If He'd said, "You'll need to sell that BMW. Oh, and that Rolex too. You're going to lose that job, and your home. I'm going to ask you to sell everything you own, and your friends are going to forget you. I'm going to ask you to move half-way around the world to serve Me in a dangerous place…," well…I probably would have run away screaming.

And so, He reveals just what I can handle at the time. It isn't because He withholds, it's because He protects.

Let's talk about faith...again

A s we became more and more comfortable with conversational prayer, Aimee and I became very successful with the same. It got to the point where we'd barely get the question out, and God would give both of us the exact same answer.

It was great.

We were praying all the time.

Our finances were great, our ministry was great. We had peace and harmony in our marriage...until we stopped hearing, that is.

We prayed, we fasted, and we asked God to reveal sin in our lives.

After a couple weeks, we were at our wits' end. In exasperation, I cried out to God in total surrender. He answered:

[you've quit living by faith]

I was stunned. God was absolutely right. We'd quit living by faith, and only did what we were told to do, when we were told to do it.

We'd gotten lazy. We wanted easy.

God wanted character.

We had to re-learn to live by faith. We learned to do the things we knew God wanted from us without express instructions. And we matured in our faith just as God intended.

What outreach looks like...now

I remember one guy I was working with. I argued with him for weeks but he was very well-trained. Also (dare I say it?), he was smarter than me. As a matter of fact, he would often teach classes on how to convert Christians to his religion.

As the days wore on with our debates, crowds began to form to watch the spectacle.

After one particularly painful exchange, I went home defeated. He had given me a list called "The 99 errors in the Bible." I had reviewed them, researched them, and refuted them. All the crowd did was laugh. When I got home, I pored over websites trying to find the very best augments against those accusations. I even found one website with a list called, "The 99 errors in the Quran."

That night, I couldn't sleep. I reviewed the exchange in my mind.

Him: "How do you explain the numerical errors between 1 Kings and 1 Chronicles?"

Me: "Well, if you take the passage in context you see that one author often mentions the entire army. This is why he says there are 15,000 soldiers. The other author only ever mentions the infantry (not mounted soldiers or the archers). This is why he says there were 5,000 troops."

Crowd: Laughter.

I cried out to God, "God, why did I lose this debate? I have the Truth, why did I lose?"

[what did it sound like]

I replied, "What?"

[what did it sound like]

I had no idea what God was talking about. I mulled it over. After at least an hour, I got it.

"God", I replied, "My reply sounded like a lie to them. Which is why they laughed."

[why would you use a something that sounds like a lie to defend the Truth?]

I had no response for that. Looking back, it was because I wanted to 'win' the argument.

After a while, I heard:

[say what I tell you tomorrow]

The next day, I was incredibly nervous. When I showed up there was a huge crowd. He came up to me, greeted me kindly, but still had a look of triumph in his eye.

"So", he said, "How about that list?"

I stood there frozen. I didn't know what to say.

The crowd began to murmur. I heard a laugh.

Suddenly, the following phrases came to me, and I spoke them softly, "You know, last night, I went on the internet trying to find a way to refute your list. I found a website with a list called, 'The 99 errors in the Quran.'"

The crowd gasped.

"But as I read it, I realized the author was writing out of hate and bitterness. There was no love."

I stepped forward, "He couldn't have been a believer, because a believer would never write with hate like that. Especially, when we know from Scripture that God is Love."

> *I asked him, "Are you a believer?"*
>
> *He replied, softly, "Yes."*
>
> *"Then", I said, looking into his eyes, "Let's put aside the arguments of unbelievers, come together as believers, and see what the Injil (Gospels) have to say."*

God accomplished in five minutes what I couldn't do with all of my arguments, training or research over a couple months.

This is what your ministry could look like.

Now, because we don't argue, people invite us over to talk about God. They invite themselves over to our house. We are jam-packed with outreach opportunities because we don't try to *do* anything.

We just show up, are obedient, introduce people to God, and get out of the way.

Once, a friend came over. I told him some of these stories. He was very nice, but with all of his experience in ministry, I could tell he was having a hard time believing me.

I said, "Want to see it in action?"

He nodded, and we walked over to the park next door.

I prayed, "God please give us a divine appointment, in Jesus' name."

Soon a family came to the park who were clearly from another country. Within two minutes we were talking about God, they invited us to their home, and we are currently doing outreach with them.

Your outreach can be effortless like this.

Remember, nothing silences an Atheist/Buddhist/Hindu/Muslim quicker than hearing from God directly. Don't debate. Simply ask them if they want to hear from God. If they do, put your hand on their shoulder and say:

> *"God, this is Bill. He needs to know you're real. In Jesus' name would you speak to him right now?"*

Then get out of the way.

What marriage looks like...now

Look, the beginning of our marriage was rough. I'm not going to lie. It's not like the institution comes with a manual or something.

Our biggest problem was our roles. So, in the US, she's supposed to be independent, smart, confident, witty, and sexy and who knows what else. I'm supposed to lead, but gently (whatever that means), provide and protect. On top of this we are both supposed to be opinionated and equals. How's that going to work?

We'll the truth is, I had it easy compared to some of my friends. My wife is genuinely a nice person, and we still had conflict.

We worked very, very hard at our marriage. But things changed about 6 years ago, and boy, I was not expecting how much.

Once we started hearing from God, we started talking to God about the things we disagreed on. Number of kids? No problem. How to spend our money? No problem. Bedroom stuff? No problem. Quit a job (or not)? No problem.

All of these things we brought before God, and He answered us.

At the same time. With the same answer. And it was never, ever wrong.

Seriously.

I lead her to God in prayer. Then, we both hear. She's in submission to God (as am I). We are in alignment, and everything works as it should. I love her, and she respects me.

There's not much left to argue about.

It's kinda simple, really. Almost like it was designed that way.

Patience and pursuing God

ne thing we've learned throughout this process is that God is on His own schedule. Often it may feel like He is stalling for no reason; at other times it seems like there is a sense of urgency we just don't get.

Looking back, we can now view major life events that He orchestrated perfectly down to the last detail. We couldn't understand it then, but we get it now.

We've seen people discouraged by their perceived failure with conversational prayer, only to have them reverse their position twenty-four hours later.

I'm left with this thought: "*Why are we in such a rush?*"

I've watched people who spent twenty years doing everything they could to ignore God throw a fit because He didn't answer their question about something relatively minor after five minutes of prayer.

Let me be clear: conversational prayer is not magic. Magic serves the practitioner as it enslaves them. God asks us to serve Him as He frees us.

God does not serve us, we serve Him. He can speak at His pleasure, in His time. We'd do well to accept that fact.

Submit yourselves therefore to God. Resist the devil, and he will flee from you. Draw near to God, and he will draw near to you. Cleanse your hands, you sinners, and purify your hearts, you double-minded. Be wretched and mourn and weep. Let your laughter be turned to mourning and your joy to gloom. Humble yourselves before the Lord, and he will exalt you.[68]

---

[68] James 4:7-10

Fasting

T his part is simple: fasting amplifies prayer. I don't know why, except to say that we are told to do it, and I've seen it work.

If you are struggling to hear from God, fast.

> *Now in the church at Antioch there were prophets and teachers: Barnabas, Simeon called Niger, Lucius of Cyrene, Manaen (who had been brought up with Herod the tetrarch) and Saul. While they were worshiping the Lord and fasting, the Holy Spirit said, "Set apart for me Barnabas and Saul for the work to which I have called them." So after they had fasted and prayed, they placed their hands on them and sent them off.*[69]

I won't get in to specifics because there are plenty of resources available on this topic. But I will mention that your fast should be a real sacrifice. It should be private, and I personally do it in twenty-four hour increments. You should fast as God leads.

If you don't hear, fast more.

---

[69] Acts 13:1-3

Doctrinal questions

I used to love doctrinal questions. Nothing would pique my interests like a good debate. Calvinism versus Armenianism. Pre-, peri- or post-tribulation. Creationism. All subjects were on the table. But that's all in the past now.

Since I have started hearing from God, all of this debate has stopped. I flat-out won't discuss it.

Here's why: I've only seen these questions divide, not unify.

Now, this is just in my case. And, I'm sure there are people who are smarter than I whose job it is to preserve these doctrinal nuances in all of their complexities.

But, it's not my job.

I have a simpler task. I introduce people to Christ. I teach them to hear from God. I get out of the way.

And...God has never answered my questions on any of these topics, so how can I speak with any authority?

Postscript

I hesitated a long time to write this workbook. There are quite a few reasons for this. Of course, it's tough writing about personal things. I worried you'd think I thought I had it all "dialed in." Then, when you met a fat, bald, grouchy little man you'd be disappointed. Maybe you'd even judge me.

Then I realized God doesn't care about any of that. And, our prayer ministry simply exploded. We couldn't keep up with all of the people who wanted to pray with us, and we needed a way to pass along our experiences without needing to meet face-to-face.

In spite of all of my reservations and excuses, God told me to write this work book.

I still have concerns, however.

First, I am very concerned about the misuse of conversational prayer. And, the potential for misuse is very, very real. An individual not properly submitted to God through Christ (with strong emotions surrounding an issue) may convince themselves that they heard from Him when they did not. I have seen this. I have seen individuals leave a marriage and say God told them to do it.

God will never contradict Himself or Scripture. As you complete these exercises; follow through on what you've heard, compare it to Scripture, test the spirit, and seek Godly counsel. Don't *ever* trust your feelings. As Scripture says, "The heart is deceitful above all things and beyond cure. Who can understand it?"[70]

Second, I am concerned that a "to-do list" of bullet points will actually limit people in their walk with Christ. This work book is brief by design and it's certainly not all-inclusive. My wife and I continue to learn from each person with whom we work, and this text merely outlines what we have learned up to this point.

Please use this as a starting point only, and allow the Holy Spirit to guide you in your own unique way of practicing conversational prayer with Him.

May our Lord bless you, and keep you. May He make His face to shine upon you, and give you peace.

---

[70] Jeremiah 17:9

About the Author

A few years ago, I had the opportunity to be mentored through an internship program at our church. During that time, we were asked to do a certain amount of outreach each week.

This internship revolutionized my outlook. It transformed my passion for Christ, His Kingdom, and it developed in me a sincere desire to reach people in a culturally appropriate way.

One recurring question I face is this: "If the things we talk about are different than the things Christ talked about, why is this?"

Because of that question, we have changed how we talk to people about Christ. No longer do we follow a script. We don't use bullet points. We simply invite people to hear from a living God, a loving Father. We make the introduction, and then get out of the way.

What if ministry could be a joy? What if it wasn't a chore, argument or debate? What if you just had to be yourself and make introductions?

This is possible with Christ.

We are currently preparing to move overseas to meet Christ there, to be Christ to those who don't know Him, and to reach the lost. We'll do our best to do this in a culturally appropriate way.

If you feel God has asked you to partner with us in either prayer or financial support, you may reach us at the following e-mail address: sent@generalmail.com . While this e-mail is secure, we do ask that you use discretion when e-mailing us for security reasons.

'Jonathan Dillon' is a pen name.

Notes

Made in the USA
Lexington, KY
31 January 2012